Chris Paul

By Jeff Savage

AMAZING ATHLETES

Lerner Publications Company • Minneapolis

For Bailey Savage, who shares his birthday with Chris Paul

Lerner Publications Company
A division of Lerner Publishing Group, Inc.
241 First Avenue North
Minneapolis, MN 55401 U.S.A.

Website address: www.lernerbooks.com

Library of Congress Cataloging-in-Publication Data

Savage, Jeff, 1961–
      Chris Paul / by Jeff Savage.
         p.   cm. — (Amazing athletes)
      Includes bibliographical references and index.
      ISBN 978-0-7613-4254-0 (lib. bdg. : alk. paper)
      1. Paul, Chris, 1985– —Juvenile literature. 2. Basketball players—United States—Biography—
   Juvenile literature. I. Title.
   GV884.P376S28 2010
   796.323'092—dc22 [B]   2008048724

Manufactured in the United States of America
1 2 3 4 5 6 – BP – 15 14 13 12 11 10

TABLE OF CONTENTS

Chris Paul dribbles around Tony Parker of the San Antonio Spurs.

HORNETS BUZZING

Chris Paul kept the basketball low. Tony Parker guarded him tightly. The sellout crowd of 17,927 fans at New Orleans Arena stood cheering. The hometown Hornets trailed in the game. Chris kept his cool. He darted past

Parker in a blur. He moved down the lane to lure the San Antonio Spurs **defenders** toward him. He fired a pass to Peja Stojakovic, who was wide open. Stojakovic drilled a **three-point basket**. Chris's smart play had given New Orleans the lead.

Chris's teammate Peja Stojakovic puts up a shot.

The Hornets and Spurs were playing the second game of the 2008 National Basketball Association (NBA) **Western Conference semifinals**. The Hornets had taken the first game with a frantic come-from-behind win. They were trying to do it again.

Chris dribbled up the court again. He made a quick **crossover** move. He drove through three defenders to the basket for a **layup**. Moments later, Chris threw another crisp pass to Stojakovic who sank a **jumper**. Soon the Hornets led, 54–43.

The Spurs were the NBA champions the year before. They were not easy to beat. Spurs star Tim Duncan made a pair of **dunks**. Chris responded. He drilled a 15-footer and then a three-pointer. On the next two Hornets plays, the Spurs **fouled** him. Chris made all four of his **free throws**. With the clock ticking down to end the third **quarter**, Chris made one more play. He dribbled through the defense and put a floating shot off the backboard for another basket. The Hornets were ahead, 78–61.

Chris is just six feet tall and 175 pounds. He is small for a pro basketball player. But Chris plays with a lot of heart. He uses his speed to control the game. He outsmarts his **opponents**. "On this team there is no doubt that Chris is the guy," Stojakovic says. "We look to Chris on every play."

Chris reaches past Tim Duncan for a shot.

Chris kept his team ahead in the fourth quarter. He finished the game with 30 points and 12 **assists**. He held the speedy Parker to just 11 points. The Hornets won easily, 102–84. "These are some of the best moments of my life," Chris said afterward. "We are just riding a wave."

Chris and his teammates celebrate their win.

Winston-Salem is located in the northern part of North Carolina.

EVERYONE'S FRIEND

Christopher Emmanuel Paul was born on May 6, 1985, in Winston-Salem, North Carolina. He grew up in nearby Lewisville. His father, Charles, builds camera equipment. His mother, Robin, works at a bank. His older brother, C.J., played basketball at the University of South Carolina. Chris's initials are C.P. His father and brother have those same initials. Charles's nickname is CP1. C.J. is CP2. Chris is CP3.

Chris was friendly and polite at school.

Chris's parents taught him good manners. They also taught him to stand up for himself. In school, Chris was an excellent student. Teachers said he was respectful. But when Chris disagreed with someone, he would "give you a look like he wanted to run you over."

Chris was a star quarterback in football. At the age of 10, he led his Pop Warner team to the national championship game in Texas. In basketball, he helped his 14-and-under team to three national tournaments. But as a high school **freshman**, Chris stood just five feet tall. The coach wanted taller players on the court.

Chris was forced to sit and watch. "I didn't like not playing," Chris said.

Chris was still just five feet two the next year. He dreamed of somehow growing taller. He played basketball every day in his backyard. "My big brother and his friends picked on me a lot," Chris said. "But I was always ready to stand up for myself." By his third year of high school, he had grown to five feet eight. He stood next to his mother in the kitchen one day, stretched to his full height, and said, "I've got you now."

Chris's favorite sport has always been basketball.

In high school, Chris faced tough competition. In this game, he played against future NBA player LeBron James (*on right*).

Chris earned straight A's at West Forsyth High School in Clemmons. He was everyone's friend. "Some students are jocks, some are nerds, some are skateboarders," the school principal said. "Chris could talk with any of them." Chris was voted president of his class every year.

As a senior, Chris starred at **point guard**. He dribbled like a wizard. He made perfect passes to teammates. In one game, he scored 37 points. Colleges **recruited** him. He agreed to attend nearby Wake Forest University.

One night, Chris received terrible news. His grandfather, Nathaniel Jones, had been killed.

Chris idolized Toussaint Lavigne, a great street basketball player. One day, Chris was lucky enough to meet Lavigne. Lavigne showed Chris how to perform a crossover dribble.

Jones was robbed and beaten to death by five teenagers. Chris deeply felt the loss of his grandfather. In his next game, Chris scored 61 points, one point for every year of his grandfather's life. When he reached 61 points, Chris missed a free throw on purpose. He then asked his coach to remove him from the game. Chris sat on the bench and cried.

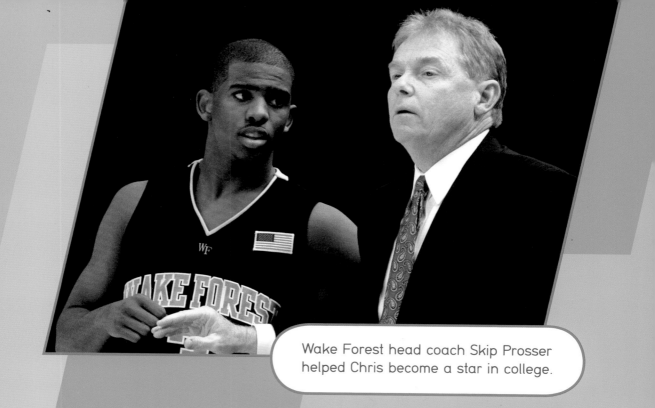

Wake Forest head coach Skip Prosser helped Chris become a star in college.

STEPPING UP

In 2003, Chris arrived at Wake Forest ready to learn. He had been voted North Carolina's Mr. Basketball as the best high school player in the state. But Chris knew playing major college basketball was a big step up. Wake Forest coach Skip Prosser prepared Chris. He gave him tapes of superstar point guard Steve Nash. Chris watched the tapes. He studied how Nash controlled a game.

Chris was an instant star. He led Wake Forest in assists, steals, three-point shooting, and free-throw shooting. He scored 10 points or more in 20 games. He broke five school records for freshmen. Wake Forest reached the National Collegiate Athletic Association (NCAA) Tournament and won its first two games. In the **Sweet 16**, Wake Forest lost to St. Joseph's. The next day, Chris called Coach Prosser to thank him for recruiting him.

Chris takes a shot against a St. Joseph's defender.

Chris taps the ball into the basket during a game against the University of Texas.

Chris's next season was even better. That year, Wake Forest was among the top ten teams in the nation! Chris led the Atlantic Coast Conference (ACC) in steals and was second in assists. He was honored as a first-team **All-America** selection. Wake Forest did not win the national title, but they did win 48 games in Chris's two years. Chris had a blast in college. But he decided to leave early. He knew it was time for him to step up one more level.

The New Orleans Hornets had the fourth overall pick in the 2005 NBA **draft**. They selected Chris. They gave him jersey number 3 for his nickname CP3. They signed him to a **contract** worth millions of dollars.

Chris smiles after the Hornets picked him in the draft.

Chris coaches at a basketball clinic for young people.

Chris quickly started spending lots of the money to help others. He rebuilt recreational basketball courts in the Winston-Salem area. He created youth basketball clinics, bowling tournaments, and other events in North Carolina and New Orleans. "I truly love this city," Chris said of his new hometown of New Orleans. "I love everything about it."

Then in August of 2005, disaster struck. Hurricane Katrina hit New Orleans! Powerful winds and rain nearly destroyed the city. Almost 2,000 people died. It was the deadliest U.S. hurricane in 77 years. Thousands of people were flooded from their homes. New Orleans Arena was used as a **shelter**. The Hornets had to leave town.

Chris is good friends with New Orleans Saints football superstar Reggie Bush. Chris and Reggie live in the same apartment building. They even share a personal chef.

Chris takes the ball to the basket in a game against the Washington Wizards.

All Ears

The Hornets played the next two seasons in Oklahoma City. Chris wanted to help his new team right away. Before the 2005–2006 season started, Chris asked Hornets coach Byron Scott for the team's playbook. "Chris memorized it in one week," Coach Scott said. "He knew everybody's spot on every play."

Chris was a star as a **rookie**. He hustled at both ends of the court. Against the Atlanta Hawks, he had 25 points, 12 assists, 7 **rebounds**, and 5 steals. He had 17 points, 12 rebounds, 9 assists, and 5 steals against the San Antonio Spurs. "Most rookies think they know it all," said Hornets player P. J. Brown. "Chris is all ears and no mouth. Everybody around here likes him."

Midway through the year in a game against the Washington Wizards, Chris scored 28 points. The next night against the New York Knicks, he had 27 points, 13 assists, and 7 rebounds. Knicks coach Larry Brown said, "He's as good as we've had come into our league in a long, long time." Chris led all NBA players in steals. He ranked seventh in assists. He led all rookies in points, assists, and steals. He was an easy choice for league Rookie of the Year!

Chris was amazing again in the 2006–2007 season. He scored 35 points against the Minnesota

Chris holds his Rookie of the Year award.

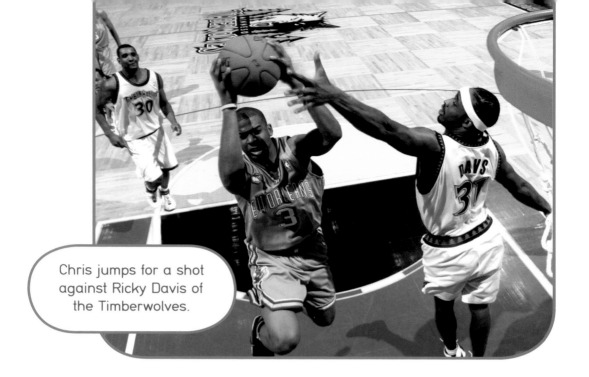

Chris jumps for a shot against Ricky Davis of the Timberwolves.

Timberwolves, his best yet. He had 18 assists against the Chicago Bulls. Opponents could not stop him. "I always try to be one step ahead of my defender," Chris explained. "I'm trying to make the guy think I'm going right, but the whole time I'm going left." Chris led the Hornets in points, assists, and steals. He did not care about his scores. He wanted to help his team reach the **playoffs**.

Chris became the leader of his team in just his third season.

SOARING HIGH

Chris was wildly popular. Before the 2007–2008 season began, he was named team captain. He was put on the cover of the NBA 2K8 video game. The Hornets were excited to return home to New Orleans, and they hoped Chris could lead them to the playoffs.

Chris took charge. He dished out 21 assists against the Los Angeles Lakers. He scored 43 points against the Memphis Grizzlies. Chris made the Hornets winners.

Fans voted Chris in as a starter for the 2008 NBA All-Star Game. The game was held at the Hornets' New Orleans Arena. The home crowd cheered loudly for Chris. He had 16 points, 14 assists, and 5 steals to lead the Western Conference. But the East held on to win the game, 134–128.

Chris goes up for a shot during the NBA All-Star Game.

Chris focused on the rest of the regular season. He had a **scoring average** of more than 21 points per game and led the NBA in assists and steals. He finished second to Kobe Bryant in the voting for league Most Valuable Player. He helped the Hornets win 56 games, the most in team history!

Chris soared high in the playoffs. The Hornets played the Dallas Mavericks in the first round. In Game 1, Chris scored 35 points to lead the Hornets to a 104–92 win. He scored 32 points and had a team playoff record of 17 assists in a 127–103 victory in Game 2. The teams each won one of the next two games. In Game 5, Chris had 24 points, 11 rebounds, and 15 assists to carry New Orleans to a 99–94 win. The Hornets moved ahead to the second round!

New Orleans faced the San Antonio Spurs next. Each team won three games. The winner

Chris goes to the hoop during a playoff game against Dallas.

of Game 7 would make it to the conference finals. Chris played great, but the Hornets lost, 91–82.

The Hornets are excited about their future with Chris. After the season, he was rewarded with a new contract. He will be paid $68 million to play at least four more years for the Hornets. Chris continues to share his money. He is one of most generous athletes in sports. *Sports Illustrated* magazine even published a story titled "Everybody Loves Chris."

Chris played point guard for Team USA in the 2008 Olympic Games. The United States won each of its first seven games by about 30 points or more. In the gold medal game, the Americans defeated Spain, 118–107. Chris made nine free throws in the game. Team USA led by just four points late in the game, but Chris sank three free throws in the final minute to help clinch the win. Chris led Team USA with 33 assists in the Olympics and was second in steals with 18. He was even sixth in rebounds despite being the shortest player on the team.

Off the basketball court, Chris is polite. On it, he works hard to win. That is what makes him great. "I can't stand to lose," Chris says. "Even today, I will be playing one-on-one against my cousin, who is 11 years old. I will let him have his fun, but in the end, I'm going to win. That's just the way it is."

Selected Career Highlights

2008–2009   Chosen as starting point guard for 2009 All-Star Team
Named Western Conference Player of the Week for the third
  week in December
Played point guard for Team USA in the 2008 Olympic Games

2007–2008   Finished second in NBA Most Valuable Player voting
Led NBA in assists
Led NBA in steals
Led Hornets to best record in team history

2006–2007   Ranked fourth in NBA in assists
Led Hornets in total points, assists, and steals

2005–2006   Named NBA Rookie of the Year
Ranked first in NBA in total steals
Ranked third in NBA in steals per game
Ranked seventh in NBA in assists per game
Led all NBA rookies in points, assists, and steals

2004–2005   Named to NCAA All-America first team
Named to Atlantic Coast Conference first team
Led Atlantic Coast Conference in steals per game (2.4)
Second in Atlantic Coast Conference in assists
  per game (6.6)

2003–2004   Led Wake Forest in assists (183), steals
  (84), three-point shooting (.465), and
  free-throw shooting (.843)
Set five Wake Forest freshman records
Named National Freshman of the
  Year by several publications

2002–2003   Named North Carolina's
  Mr. Basketball
Named to McDonald's All-
  America first team
Led West Forsyth High School in
  per game scoring (30.8), assists
  (9.5), and steals (6)

Glossary

All-America: a group of the top college players in the nation

assists: passes to teammates that help those teammates score baskets

contract: a written deal between a player and a team

crossover: a dribbling move in which a player shifts direction while moving the ball from one hand to the other

defenders: players who try to stop the other team from scoring

draft: a yearly event in which professional sports teams take turns choosing new players from a selected group

dunks: scoring by slamming the basketball through the hoop

fouled: to be hit, touched, or pushed by an opponent in a way that is against the rules

free throws: a shot from behind the free throw line. Players often get to shoot free throws after being fouled.

freshman: first year of high school or college

jumper: a play in which the player jumps and shoots the ball at a distance from the basket

layup: a shot from under the basket

opponents: players on the other team

playoffs: a series of games to decide the league's champion

point guard: a basketball player whose job it is to dribble and pass the ball

quarter: part of a game. There are four quarters in each basketball game.

rebounds: basketballs grabbed after missed shots

recruited: offered a position to play for a college team, in exchange for normal costs of attending the school

rookie: a player in his or her first pro season

scoring average: a number that describes how many points a player usually scores per game

semifinals: the second round of the NBA playoffs. The winner of the semifinals series goes on to the conference finals.

shelter: a safe place with food and supplies where people can go in an emergency

Sweet 16: the final 16 teams competing in the yearly NCAA tournament

three-point basket: a long-range shot that counts for three points

Western Conference: one of two conferences that make up the NBA. The 15-team Western Conference includes the Dallas Mavericks, Minnesota Timberwolves, New Orleans Hornets, and San Antonio Spurs.

Further Reading & Websites

Gilbert, Sara. *The Story of the New Orleans Hornets.* Mankato, MN: Creative Education, 2007.

Kennedy, Mike, and Mark Stewart. *Swish: The Quest for Basketball's Perfect Shot.* Minneapolis: Millbrook Press, 2009.

Paul, Chris. *Long Shot: Being Small Doesn't Mean You Can't Dream Big.* New York: Simon & Schuster, 2009.

Savage, Jeff. *LeBron James.* Minneapolis: Lerner Publications Company, 2006.

Savage, Jeff. *Tim Duncan.* Minneapolis: Lerner Publications Company, 2010.

Chris Paul, the Official Website
http://www.chrispaul3.com
Chris's official website features news, records, photos, trivia, and other information about Chris and his team.

Official NBA Site
http://www.nba.com
The official National Basketball Association website provides fans with game results, statistics, schedules, and biographies of players.

Sports Illustrated Kids
http://www.sikids.com
The *Sports Illustrated Kids* website covers all sports, including basketball.

Index

Photo Acknowledgments

The images in this book are used with the permission of: © Layne Murdoch/
NBAE via Getty Images, pp. 4, 5, 7; © Chris Graythen/Getty Images, p. 8;
© age fotostock/SuperStock, p. 9; Seth Poppel Yearbook Library, p. 10;
© Linda Spillers/WireImage.com, p. 11; REUTERS/Gary Hershorn, p. 12; AP
Photo/Frank Franklin II, p. 14; AP Photo/Al Behrman, p. 15; AP Photo/Chuck
Burton, p. 16; AP Photo/Kathy Willens, p. 17; AP Photo/The Oklahoman,
Chris Lansberger, p. 18; © Mitchell Layton/NBAE via Getty Images, p. 20; AP
Photo/Bill Haber, p. 22; © David Sherman/NBAE via Getty Images, p. 23;
© Andrew D. Bernstein/NBAE via Getty Images, p. 24; © Jesse D. Garrabrant/
NBAE/Getty Images, p. 25; © Glenn James/NBAE via Getty Images, p. 27;
© D. Clarke Evans/NBAE via Getty Images, p. 29.

Front Cover: © Bill Baptist/NBAE via Getty Images.